TOP 40 1995

Arrangements by WAYNE HAUN
Edited by SYLVIA MAYS and JAMES R.
Typesetting by GARY TUCKER for Heartsong Mus

INDEX

MOST OF ALL

Words and Music
Carroll McGruder

C
F/C
F
C
all I want to look up- on the Mas- ter, And sing prais- es when at
C
G
C
last the bat - tle's won; I want to know I've run the
C7
F
Fm
Fm6
C/G
race, Hear Je - sus say I've kept the faith, And most of all I want to
G7
C
1.
C
2.
hear Him say well done. done.

I WILL RISE UP FROM MY GRAVE

Words and Music
Jack and Gail Toney

CHORUS
A♭
A♭/E♭
D♭/E♭
A♭
I will rise up to meet Him in the sky,
A♭
E♭7
On that home - com - ing morn - ing by and by,
D♭/E♭
A♭
A♭/C
D♭
A♭
When the trum - pet of God be - gins to sound,
A♭
D♭
A♭/E♭
E♭7
A♭
We will rise up from the grave to meet the Lamb.

JOY ON THE OTHER SIDE OF JORDAN

Words and Music
L. Kirk Talley

CHORUS
F
B♭
F
There'll be joy on the oth-er side of Jor - dan,
B♭
C
F
Peace will last for - ev - er and a day. There'll be joy on the
B♭
F
B♭
F
oth-er side of Jor - dan; What a glor - i - ous cel - e - bra - tion far be -
B♭
F
B♭ Gm
F/C
C
F
yond i - mag - in - a - tion, There'll be joy on the oth - er side some - day.

UNLIKE ME, JUST LIKE HIM

Words and Music
Larry Petree

D♭ D♭° D♭ A♭ E♭7 A♭
cross He said, "For - give them for they know not what they do" When He
D♭ D♭° D♭ A♭ E♭7
said, "It is fin - ished" He made that pos - si - ble for you,
A♭ A♭/G♭ D♭6 D♭ D♭6 D♭ E♭
Cal-v'ry's where the ha - tred ends and for - give-ness be - gins, It's un - like
A♭ E♭7 A♭
me, but it's just like Him.

PURE MERCY

Words and Music
Bill Burns & Gary S. Paxton

D
G
mer - cy, pure me - r - cy, On a pris - on - er con-demned to
D
A
Bm
die, He had mer - cy, pure me - r - cy, I had no
D/A
D/F♯
Bm
A♯6
par - don in - side, but then Je - sus passed by, And had
D/A
Bm
1. 2.
D
3.
D
mer - cy on a sin - ner such as I. I.

GOD HAS PROVIDED A LAMB

Words and Music
John & Jason Johnson

E♭

A - bra - ham faced a moun - tain, with an un - cer - tain
At the top of the moun - tain, an al - tar they

B♭7 A♭/F

task, I - saac walked with him, for God had
made, and af - ter prep - a - ra - tions, there I - saac was

B♭7 E♭ E♭/G

asked, that a sac - ri - fice be made on an al - tar of
laid, when a voice from the heav - ens spoke to A - bra -

A♭ E♭ A♭ E♭ E♭/G Fm/A♭ E♭/B♭ B♭7

stone, fac - ing the moun - tain, A - bra - ham jour - neyed
ham, "Touch not the lad, God has pro - vid - ed a

E♭
1.
on.
E♭
2.
ram.
He pro -
Cm
A♭
E♭
vid - ed a ram, whose blood cleansed and saves, He pro -
vid - ed a Lamb, whose blood cleansed and saves, He pro -
Cm
A♭
E♭
B♭7
vid - ed a ram, and a - tone - ment was made, His
vid - ed a Lamb, and a - tone - ment was made, His
Cm
A♭
E♭
E♭/G
A♭
on - ly son I - saac, on the al - tar lay down,
on - ly son Je - sus, on the al - tar lay down,

E♭
E♭/G
Fm/A♭
E♭/B♭
Last Time To Coda
E♭
3.
God has pro - vid - ed a ram.
God has pro - vid - ed a
E♭
I once faced a moun - tain, sin was its
B♭7
A♭/F
name, with no way a - round it, years I strug - gled in
B♭7
E♭
vain, un - til I knelt at an al - tar, it was there that I

A♭ E♭ E♭/G Fm/A♭ E♭/B♭ B♭7 E♭
found, God has pro - vid - ed a Lamb.
E♭ A♭
4.
He pro -
Lamb. I stood in
E♭ A♭
judge - ment, in sin all a - lone, 'til the blood that flowed from
E♭/G A♭ B♭sus4 B♭ E♭
D.S.
He pro
Cal - va - ry, made me spot less be - fore the throne. Lamb.

I SHALL WEAR A CROWN

Traditional

Db7
Ab/Eb
Ab+5/E
Fm
To Coda
Ab/Eb
F7
Bb7
Eb7
I shall wear a crown
I shall wear a crown
I shall wear a robe and
Ab
D.S. al Coda
Ab7
Bbm/Ab
Ab
Ab7
Bbm/Ab
Ab
crown
Soon as my feet strike Zi - on, lay down my heav-y bur - den Gon-na
Db7
Ebm/Db
Db7
Ab7
Bbm/Ab
Ab
put on my robe in Glo - ry, shout and tell Him my sto - ry
Ab7
Bbm/Ab
Ab
Ab7
Bbm/Ab
Ab
Soon as I can see Je - sus, tell Him all a - bout my trou - ble
Db7
Ebm/Db
Db7
Ab
Ab7
Bbm/Ab
Ab
put on my robe in Glo - ry, shout and tell Him my sto - ry

Ab7
Bbm/Ab
Ab
Ab7
Bbm/Ab
Ab
Soon as my feet strike Zi - on, lay down my heav - y bur - den
Db7
Ebm/Db
Db7
Ab
Ab7
Bbm/Ab
Ab
Put on my robe in Glo - ry, shout and tell Him my sto - ry
Ab7
Ab
Ab7
Bbm/Ab
Ab
Soon as I can see Je - sus, tell Him all a - bout my trou - ble
Db7
Ebm/Db
Db7
Ab
Ab7
Put on my robe in Glo - ry, shout, shout, tell Him my sto - ry
Ab
F7
Bb7
Eb7
Ab
I shall wear a robe and crown

THAT'S ENOUGH

Words and Music
Roger Horne

MY SOUL PROVIDER

Words and Music
Phil Cross

A
CHORUS
D/F♯
A7/G
D/F♯
G
flow.
need.
Je - sus is my soul pro - vid - er, My
D/F♯
D/G
D
A7
D/F♯
A7/G
G
one and on - ly soul sup - pli - er, And He's made me a soul sur -
D
G
D/F♯
G
D/A
viv - er, Je - sus is my soul pro -
A7
D
D
1.
2.
vid - er. er.

BUILT ON AMAZING GRACE

Words and Music
Darryl Williams & Chris Collins

B♭
house is built on a - maz - ing grace, an-chored in the Rock of A - ges,
F7
B♭
Bought by the blood of the Lamb, re - cord-ed in the bi - ble pag - es, The
B♭
floors are ho - ly ground, and the walls are made of praise, And the
F7
F7
B♭
de - vil can't tear it down, it's built on a - maz - ing grace!

GOD KEPT HIS PROMISE

Words and Music
Jeff Steele

E E7 A E

God spoke to A - bra - ham here is your de - sire, you and your wife

F♯/C♯ B7 E E7

Sar - ah are go - ing to have a child A - bra - ham re - spond - ed we are

A E A E/B B7

old how can this be and God said I prom - ise you and Sar - ah just be -

E A E7 A B E

lieve And God kept His prom - ise He hon - ored His Word the

E A E F♯ Bsus4 B
womb that was emp - ty has now been made full and your
E A E A B E A
seed will num - ber the sands by the sea be - cause you be -
E/B B7 E
lieved God kept His prom - ise Man - y thou - sand years
E7 A E
lat - er on the hill of Cal - va - ry Je - sus was dy - ing on an

F♯
B
B+5
E
A
old rug - ged tree when He cried it is fin - ished they took His bod - y
E
A
E/B
B7
E
C
C+5
down and God's re - demp - tion prom - ise was laid in the ground Ver - y
F
F7
B♭
F
B♭
ear - ly in the morn - ing on the first day of the week came Mar - y bear - ing
F
G
C7
C+5
F
spic - es His bod - y to keep when she ar - rived at the tomb two men in

B♭ F B♭ F/C C C7
white were there to say that God kept His prom - ise and Je - sus is a - live to -
F F B♭ F B♭ C
day And God kept His prom - ise He hon - ored His
F B♭ F G G7 C7sus4
Word the tomb is emp - ty and Je - sus is Lord
C F B♭ F F7 B♭ F/A B♭/G F
He came out of the grave with pow - er to save
B♭ F/A B♭/G F/C C B♭/F F
all who be - lieve God kept His prom - ise

SHOULDER TO SHOULDER

Words and Music
Jeff Steele

A♭
D♭/A♭
A♭
A♭/F
word of the Lord to a world that with - out him is just
B♭m7
3
E♭sus4
D♭
E♭
A♭
D♭/A♭
dy - ing to hear, Let's stand broth - er to broth - er let's start
3
A♭
D♭/A♭
A♭
A♭/F
lov - ing each oth - er, and when the world sees our ac - tions they will
B♭m7
3
1. E♭sus4
2. E♭sus4 D♭/E♭ E♭7
A♭
D♭/A♭ A♭
lend an ear. ear. Let's stand shoul - der to shoul - der.
3

THREAD OF HOPE

Words and Music
Marcia Henry

CHORUS
E♭
A♭
D♭
hand.
through.
'Cause when you're hang - ing by a thread,___ Still you can climb life's
A♭
E♭
moun - tain. Though the cliffs are rough and jag - ged, you can crawl.___
A♭
D♭
___ If you should slip and reach rope's end, You'll find the hem of His
A♭
A♭/E♭
E♭
A♭
gar - ment, So don't let go of that last thread of hope.

PRAYER CHANGES ME

Words and Music
Sheryl Farris

Db
Ab
Bbm
Eb7(sus4)
whis - per a prayer that on - ly He hears, And I rest peace - ful - ly.
when I be - gin to trust more in Him, I can sing a song.
CHORUS
Eb7
F7
Bbm
Bbm7
Eb/G
Ab
Cm/G
Fm
Bbm
Bbm7
I can pray out loud or si - lent - ly, I can pray stand - ing
Eb/G
Ab
Eb7/Bb
Ab7/C
Db
Eb
Eb7
Ab
Eb/G
tall or on my knees. It real - ly makes no differ - ence, just that prayer is the
Fm
Bbm
Eb/G
Db
Eb
Ab
key. 'Cause prayer chang - es things and it chang - es me.

I'M GOING THROUGH JESUS

Words and Music
Herbert Buffam

CHORUS
G
G
through.
through.
I'm go - ing through yes,
C G G
I'm go - ing through, I'll pay the price what -
A7 Dsus4 D7 G G7
ev - er oth - ers do, I'll take the way with my
C G G G/D D7 G
Lord's despised few, I have started in Je - sus and I'm go - ing through.

HE'S GOT A MIRACLE FOR YOU

Words and Music
Bo Hinson & Ronnie Hinson

D
G
He could still the storm for His dis - ci - ples,
If
D
A
He could feed the hun - gry mul - ti tude;
D
G
turn the wa - ter in - to wine,
touch the lame and heal the blind,
D
A
A7
D
Then He's got a mir - a - cle for you.

SPEAK TO THE MOUNTAIN

Words and Music
Marcia Henry

CHORUS
A♭
A♭/E♭
D♭/E♭
A♭
A♭/E♭
D♭
pear.
feet.
Speak to the moun - tain, you'll not tri - umph o - ver
A♭
A♭
B♭7
me, be thou re - moved from here to yon - der, dis - ap - pear in - to the
E♭7
D♭/E♭
E♭
A♭
A♭7
D♭
sea, Speak to the moun - tain, speak with au - thor - it - y,
A♭/E♭
E♭7
A♭
and the moun - tain must move, and you shall claim vic - to - ry.

GOD LIKES TO WORK
(WHEN NOTHING ELSE WILL)

Words and Music
Marcia Henry and Larry Petree

D6/A A
D
G
D6/A A
work when your back's to the wall, When fate's in the bal - ance and you're
D
A7 D/F♯ D9/F♯ G
D6/A A
D
just a - bout to fall, So there'll be no mis - tak - in' when He bless - es and
G
G2
D
A7
heals, Oh, God likes to work when no - thin' else
D
D
1.
2.
will.
will.

JESUS' ROCKING CHAIR

Words and Music
Tim Greene

D D/G G

1. Man - y hope - ful Moms and Dads try to have a child of their own. Some
2. There are those who have a boy or girl, a love - ly gift from God, but
3. She was eight - een and not mar - ried, ex - pect - ing her lit - tle one, but in her

D D/B Em Asus4 A7

nev - er get the chance, oth - ers do and see them grown. There are
sick - ness or a trag - e - dy takes them from their par - ents arms. Ma - mas
time of her con - fu - sion, she took the life of her own son. Since

D F♯sus4 F♯ Bm

those who are ex - pect - ing that pre - cious ba - by soon, but it's
wish for days gone by and Dad - dys long for that lost child, but
then, Je - sus for - gave her and took all her shame a - way, but still

Em D Bm Em A7 D

gone be - fore it ev - er leaves the safe - ty of it's Ma - ma's womb.
chil - dren are not lost when you know where they are.
she cries, miss - ing her ba - by, but she hears the an - gels say.

CHORUS
D G D
Je - sus has a rock - ing chair and He
D A/C♯ Bm Em A7
holds that pre - cious ba - by with, oh, such ten - der care. He takes the
D A/C♯ Bm A/F♯ G
place of Mom and Dad, He's the great - est par - ent a child could have. Don't
G D Bm Em A7 D
wor - ry a - bout the chil - dren there, Je - sus has a rock - ing chair.

HE'S MY HIDING PLACE

Words and Music
Dee Gaskin

A♭7
D♭
And He is my sword and shield in the heat of the bat - tle,
E♭
A♭
He is my coun - sel - or and friend full of mer - cy and grace, My Je - sus is
D♭
D♭
E♭
stead - fast and true when the world stands a - gainst me, He is my
A♭
D♭
A♭/E♭
E♭7
1.2.
A♭
3.
A♭
cleft in the might - y rock, He's my hid - ing place. place.

WILT THOU BE MADE WHOLE?

Words and Music
Carroll Roberson

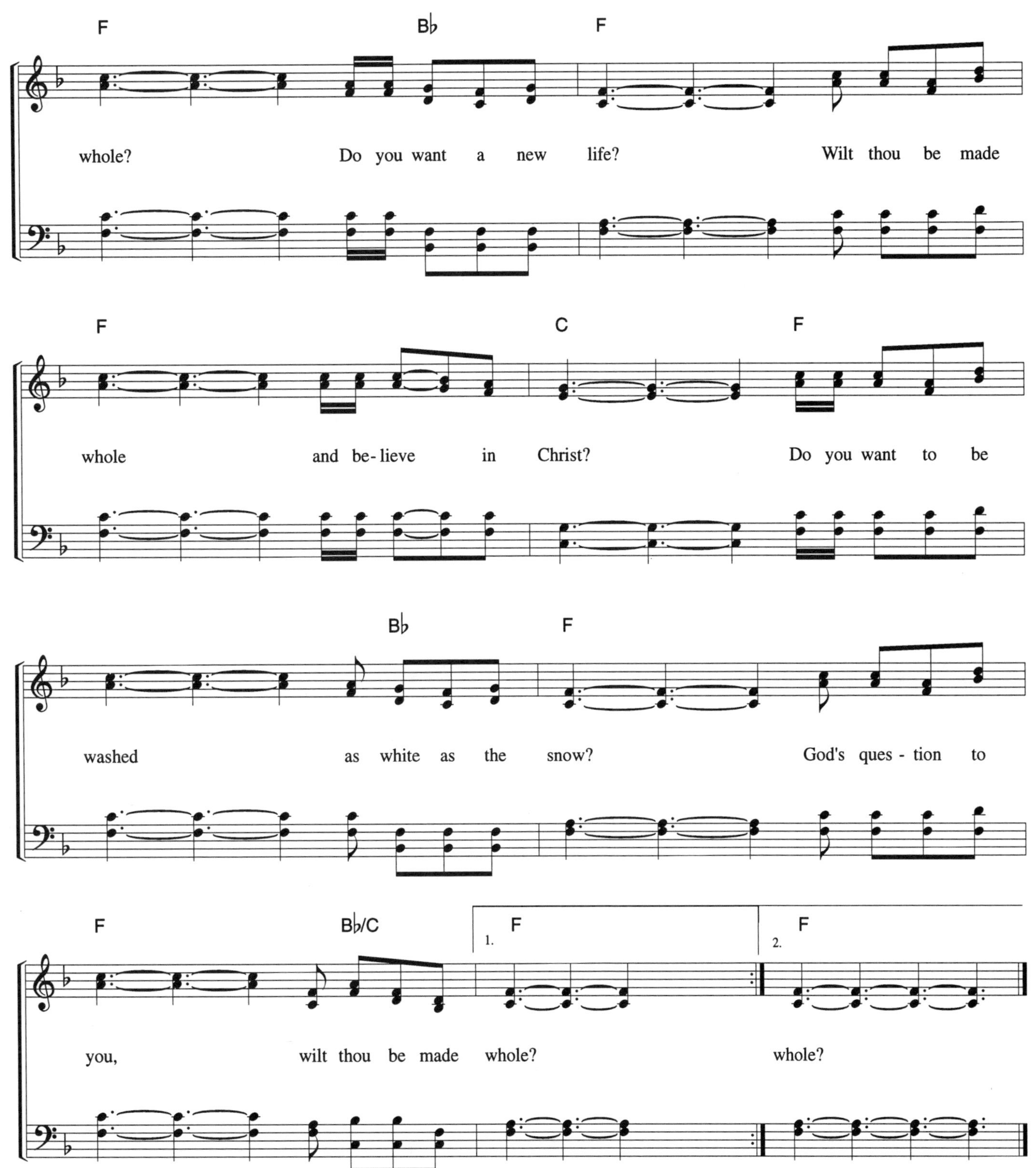
F
B♭
F
whole? Do you want a new life? Wilt thou be made
F
C
F
whole and be-lieve in Christ? Do you want to be
B♭
F
washed as white as the snow? God's ques - tion to
F
B♭/C
1.
F
2.
F
you, wilt thou be made whole? whole?

HE'LL DO IT AGAIN

Words and Music
Dawn Thomas

CHORUS
E♭7
A♭
D♭ 𝄋
A♭
And He'll do it a - gain,
He'll do it a - gain,
Fm
Fm+7
Fm7
B♭7
E♭
Just take a look at where you are now and where you've been;
E♭7
A♭
A♭/C
D♭
A♭
Has - n't He al - ways come through for you, He's the same now as then,
D♭
B♭m
A♭/E♭
E♭
E♭7
To Coda
1.
A♭
You may not know how, you may not know when, but He'll do it a - gain.

A♭
C
Fm
2.
gain.
Oh, He's still God,
Cm
Fm
and He will not fail you,
Oh, He's still God,
Cm
B♭m
and He will not change;
Just like Mo - ses, just like
A♭/C
B♭m7
A♭/D♭
E♭7
A♭
D.S. al Coda
A♭
Dan - iel, just like Sha - drach, Me - shach, A - bed - ne - go. He'll do it a - gain.
gain.

ALWAYS ENOUGH

Words and Music
Kirk Talley

CHORUS

There is al-ways e-nough of God's mer-cy, Al-ways e-nough of His love, When your well has run dry, He will sup-ply, When the road gets long and rough, There is al-ways e-nough. *Fine*

STANZAS

1. Hard cir-cum-stanc-es may haunt you, Play-in' a game which way to turn, Re-al-iz-in' right and wrong both want you, This my friend a les-son I have learned.
2. Ev'-ry-one a-round you thinks you're per-fect, 'Cause you know ex-act-ly what to say, Oh, but now the ta-ble's turned, you're the one that's hurt-ing, You're a-fraid to give your heart a-way. *D.S.*
3. But I know a place of con-so-la-tion, Where mer-cy is ex-tend-ed fresh and new, Fail-ure is-n't fi-nal with the Fa-ther, God's sea of for-give-ness flows for you. *D.C. al Fine*

RAINBOW AVENUE

Words and Music
Vern Sullivan

G7
C
F
3
ain't got a dime.
But I'm an heir to love di - vine.
3
F
B♭7/A♭
Now, let me tell you 'bout my home.
Is your home sure 'nough pret - ty?
Sure 'nough.
So fair in the
F
G
four square cit - y.
From my front porch I'll have a heav - en - ly view of Rain-bow Av - e -
C
G
C
F
nue.
Rain - bow Av - e - nue.
Well, there'll be red, white, and yel - low,

F
B♭
G7
F
brown and black folks, But
no - bod - y will be blue
In that heav - en - ly mixed up
F7
D7
G7
C
F
Fine
F
neigh - bor - hood on Rain - bow Av - e - nue.
Well, tell us
C
F
more a - bout Rain - bow Av - e - nue.
I'm gon - na be
F
F
B♭
F
mov - in', mov-in' on in.
Mov - in', mov - in' where?
Well,

F
G7
C
mov-in' on in when the saints in glo - ry, All go mov-in' in. Well
you ain't no saint, no saint you ain't, You're a mean old sin - ner
3
F
F7
D7
man. Well a sin - ner I was, but a saint I am, I was
G
G7
F
D.S. al Fine
lost but now I'm found. Now, let me tell you 'bout my

HE'LL KEEP YOU THROUGH

Words and Music
Felecia Shifflett

CHORUS

D G G/D D
through.
He'll keep you through the fi - re when it be-comes a furn - ace,
through.
A D D7
He'll keep you through the wa - ters when they be-come a flood, He would not
G D A
make what He could not keep, He did not start what he can't com - plete, What He does not keep you
A7 D 1. 2. D
from, He'll keep you through. through.

I'LL BE BACK

Words and Musi
Michael Comb

2.
Ab7 Ab/Bb Eb Cm
And af - ter they laid my sweet Je- sus in the tomb He got
just a few short days then I'll be back"
Ab Cm Ab
up and took a trip down be- low and showed the de- vil that he had lost the bat- tle for man's soul
Cm Eb/G Ab Eb/G
and I be- lieve that as He took the keys He looked the de- vil right in the eye He said, "The
Ab Ab/F Bb7 Ab/Bb Eb
grave could not hold me I'm head- ed back to Glo- ry so, de- vil, just keep this in mind I'll be back, I'll be

B♭/D
A♭
3
E♭/B♭
B♭7
E♭
back I'll be gone for a sea-son, ol' boy one day I'm com-ing back, I'll be back
3
E♭
Gm/E♭
A♭7
One day on a hill-side as Je - sus rose up in the clouds the words He spoke came flood-ing back to some
E♭/B♭
Fm/B♭
E♭
Gm/E♭
young men in the crowd He said, "I go to pre-pare a place, but I'll be back a - gain
A♭7
A♭/B♭
E♭
gon-na take my peo - ple to a land where joy shall nev - er end 'cause I'll be back,
B♭/D
A♭
E♭/B♭
A♭/B♭
E♭
I'll be back I'll just be gone for a lit-tle while one day I'm com-ing back I'll be back

OUT OF HIS GREAT LOVE

Words and Music
Terry & Barbi Franklin

G C C/D G Em G/B C D D7

I had gone a - stray I had lost my way when I called up - on His
Now I shout His praise through all my days for His end - less mer-cy and

G G/D C C/D G

name, Then He res - cued me now the song I sing,
grace, There's no oth - er one who has great - er love,

C D G

"What a lov - ing God is He."
With joy I will ev - er sing.

CHORUS

G C G

Out of His great love, He picked me up

C G D G G/B C G C

Set my feet on a sturd - y rock, Out of His great love I've learned the mean - ing of sal -

G/D D7 1 G 2. G

va - tion Out of HIs great love. love.

I GO TO THE ROCK OF AGES

Words and Music
Squire Parsons

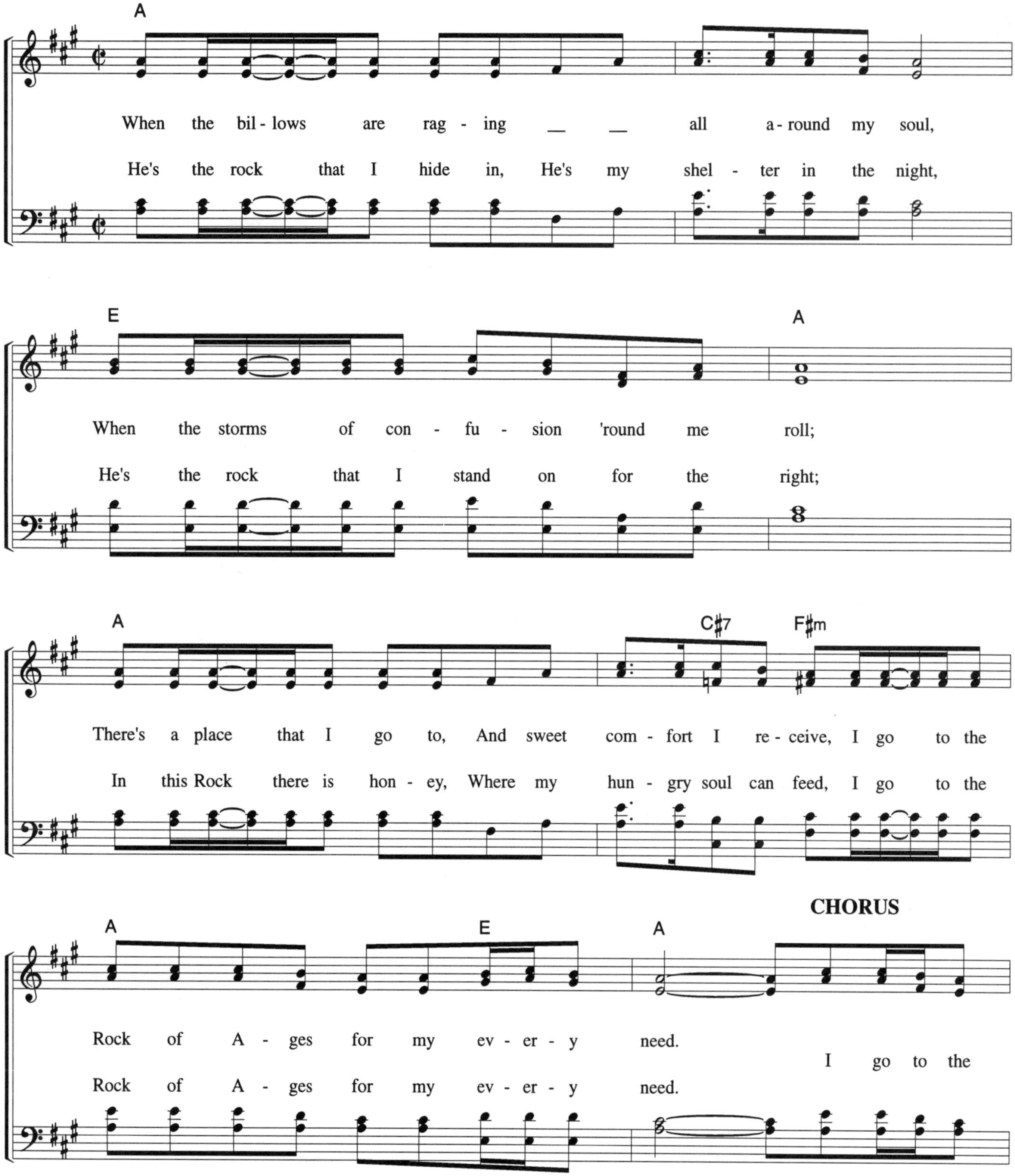
A
When the bil - lows are rag - ing __ __ all a - round my soul,
He's the rock that I hide in, He's my shel - ter in the night,
E
A
When the storms of con - fu - sion 'round me roll;
He's the rock that I stand on for the right;
A
C♯7
F♯m
There's a place that I go to, And sweet com - fort I re - ceive, I go to the
In this Rock there is hon - ey, Where my hun - gry soul can feed, I go to the
CHORUS
A
E
A
Rock of A - ges for my ev - er - y need.
I go to the
Rock of A - ges for my ev - er - y need.

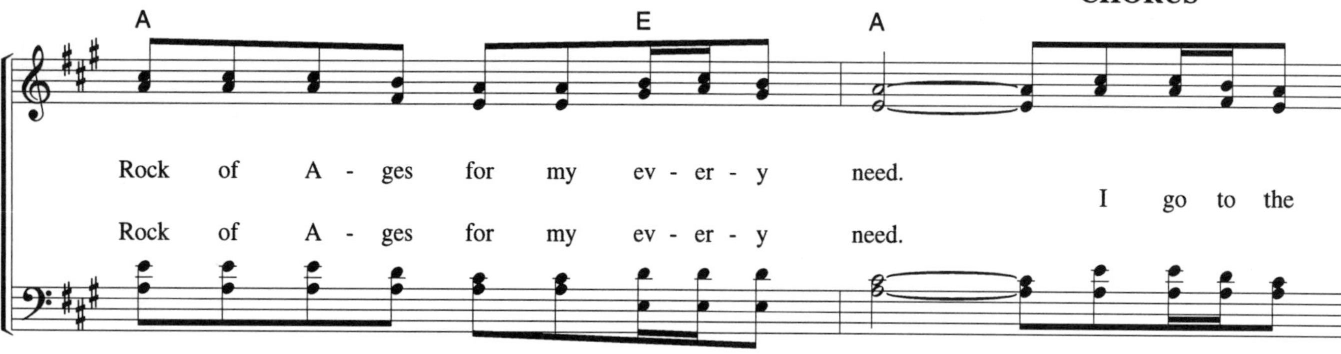

A
Rock of A - ges, I go to the
F♯m
A
E7
A
D
Rock for my ev' - ry need; When I'm dis -
A
D
A
C♯7
F♯m
cour - aged, When I am sad, I go to the Rock, He makes me glad, I go to the
A
E7
A
Rock of A - ges for my ev - er - y need.

HE MEANS THE WORLD TO ME

Words and Music

Larry and Rachel Petree

E♭
B♭
F
B♭
life was down to no-thin',___ Je - sus turned my life a - round, My___
E♭
B♭
F
F7
hopes and dreams were shat-tered,___ And ly - ing scat - tered on the ground; Oh,
B♭
F
B♭
E♭
yes I real - ly love Him___ and yet it's plain to see, He___
E♭
B♭
F
B♭
B♭
1.
2.
does-n't___ mean much to this world, But He means the world to me.
me.

MY FOOTSTEPS WILL END AT THE THRONE

Words and Music
Danny and Dee Kramer

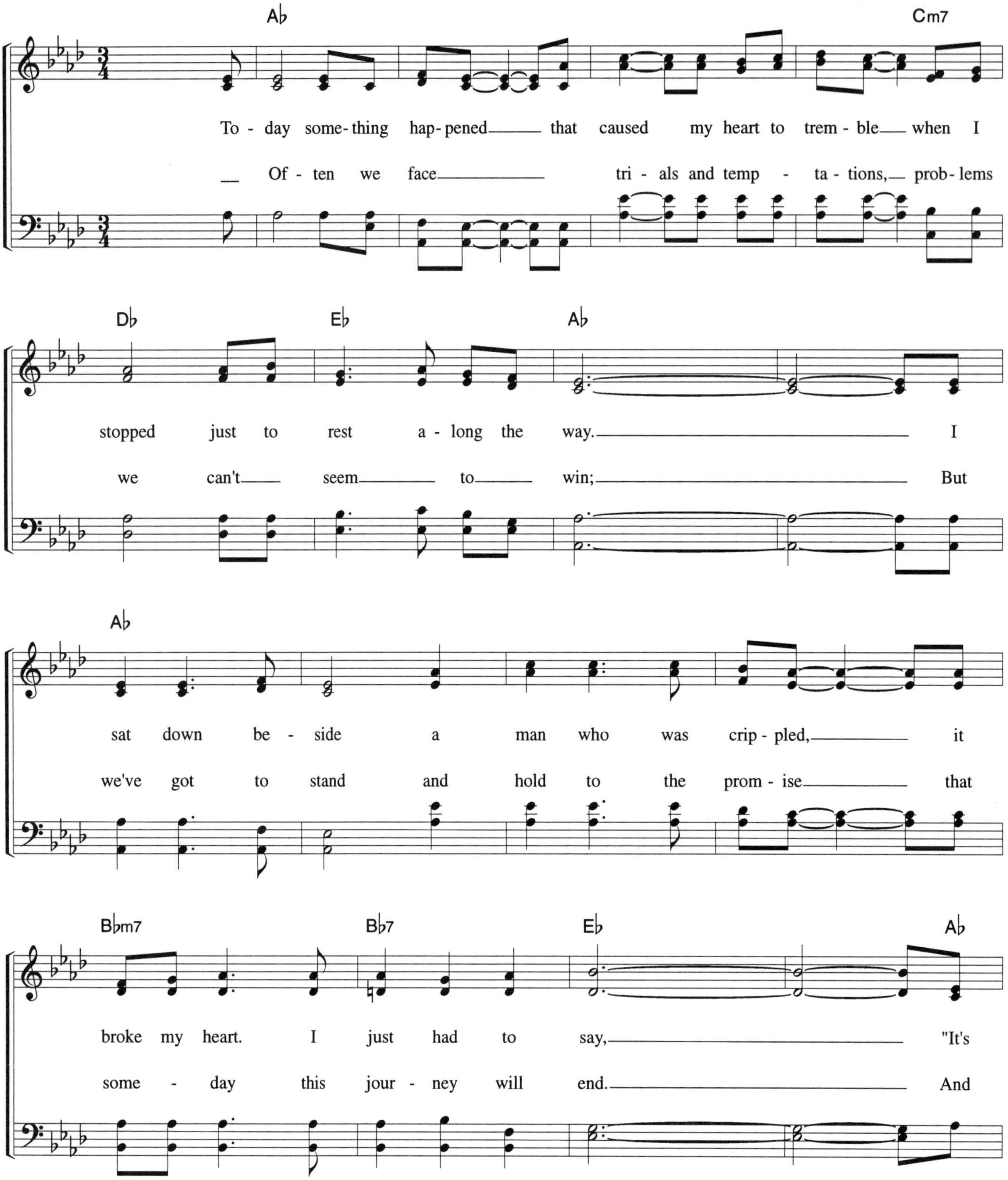

A♭ Cm7

To - day some-thing hap-pened___ that caused my heart to trem - ble___ when I
__ Of - ten we face___ tri - als and temp - ta - tions,__ prob-lems

D♭ E♭ A♭

stopped just to rest a - long the way.___ I
we can't___ seem___ to___ win;___ But

A♭

sat down be - side a man who was crip - pled,___ it
we've got to stand and hold to the prom - ise___ that

B♭m7 B♭7 E♭ A♭

broke my heart. I just had to say,___ "It's
some - day this jour - ney will end.___ And

A♭
Cm7
hard now, but some-day you're gon-na run all o-ver heav-en up and
I know when my life gets rough and rock-y, I'm
D♭
E♭
A♭
down the streets of pure gold." He
gon-na keep press-ing on, For
D♭
A♭/C
D♭
looked down and said, "No, when these feet start walk-ing, they'll be
Je-sus is wait-ing to wel-come me home, And my
A♭
E♭7
A♭
head-ed straight for the throne."
foot-steps will end at the throne.

CHORUS
D♭
A♭
Some - day I'll reach my fi - nal home, The
Fm
Fm7/E♭
B♭7
E♭
cares of this life will all be gone,
A♭/C
D♭
A♭/C
No tri - als, no heart- aches, there my jour - ney will be
D♭
A♭/E♭
E♭7
A♭
1.
A♭
2.
o'er, And my foot- steps will end at the throne. throne.

I AM

Words and Music
Terry Wilkins & Gina White

OH COME ALONG

Words and Music
Dianne Wilkinson

C
Em7 E♭m6 D7 G
long with me and go to that land, Where milk and hon - ey flow so free; God has pre -
C° C
C+ C G7
pared that cit - y with His own hand, And there's a man - sion wait - ing me. We'll spend the
C
E7 F
end - less a - ges prais - ing His name, As we sing re - demp - tion's song; Oh, we'll be
C C A9 D7 G6 G7 C
leav - ing just an - y day, Sud - den - ly called a - way, Don't stay be - hind, Oh, come a - long.

WHERE ARE THE CHILDREN?

Words and Music
Gene and Val Johnson

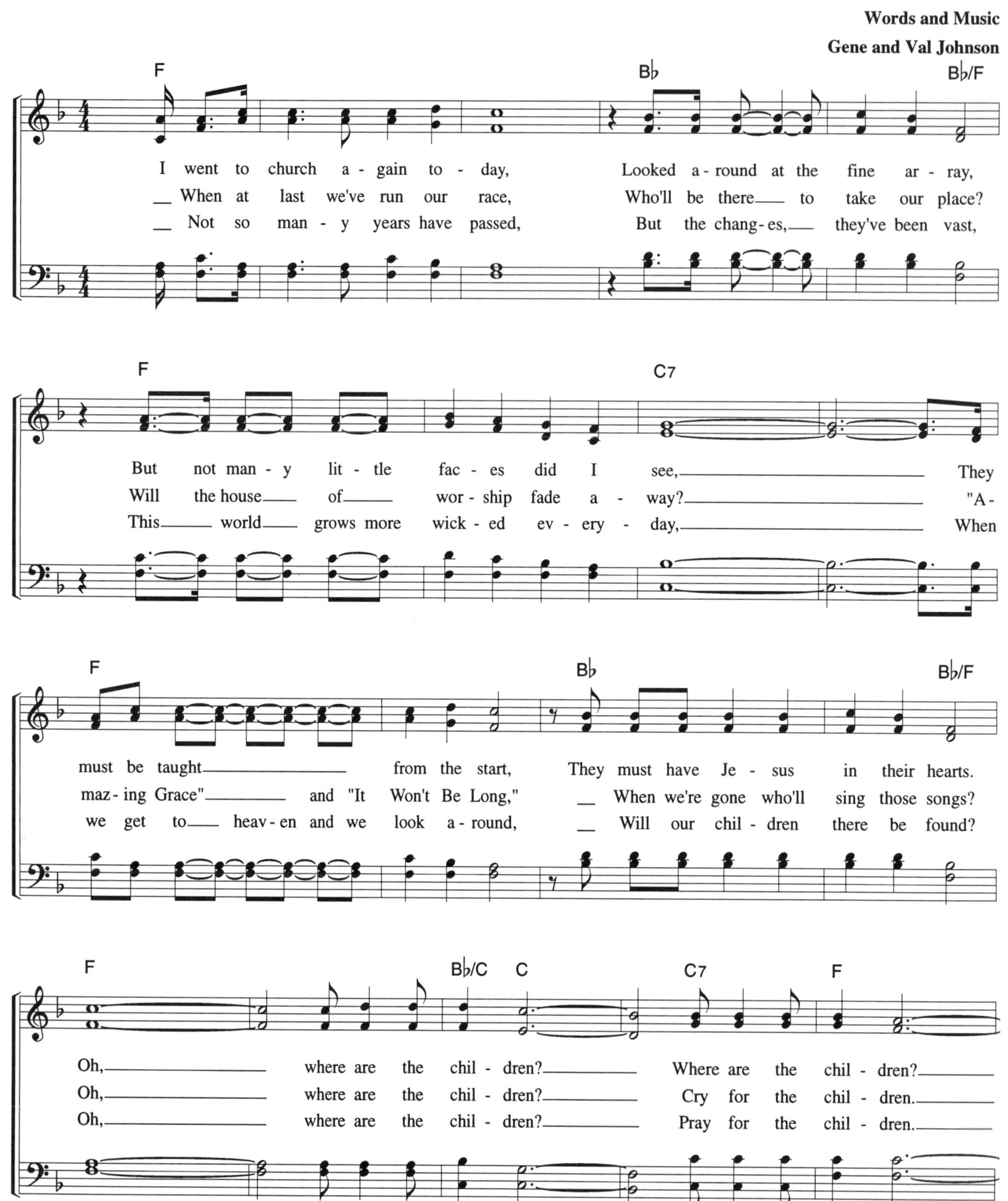

CHORUS
F
B♭
Is Sa - tan steal - ing them a - way? Are we too blind to see to - day?
F
Dm7/C C
F
Oh, where are the chil - dren? Re - mem - ber Je - sus
F
B♭
F
said it best, "When I re - turn will I find faith?" Oh, where are the
Dm7/C C
B♭
C9
F
1. 2.
3. F
chil - dren? Where are the chil - dren? dren?

I'LL BE LIVING THAT WAY

Words and Music
Carroll Roberson

C7
F
C7
walk-ing with Je - sus by my side, I'm gon - na be
F
B♭/F
F
talk - ing with my loved ones who have died,
3
3
B♭/F F
B♭9
3
I'm gon - na be sing - ing in that home of un - cloud - ed
3
B♭ F/A B♭
F
B♭
B♭7 F
day, I know that I'm gon - na be liv - ing that way.

I NEED YOU

Words and Music
Sheri Easter

Em7
C
D7
true, Ev - en when I've turned my back on You.
ry, And I know You're all I'll ev - er need.
G
Bridge
C
G
C
gain. You've giv - en ev - ery - thing I could ev - er ask for, A home and a fam - i - ly and
D7
3
G
D7
G
so much more. I need You like flow - ers need the sun - shine, I need You like trees need the rain,
3
G
D7
G
I need You more now than ev - er, Lord, I need Your touch a - gain.

JESUS HAS RISEN

Words and Music
Dianne Wilkinson

CHORUS
E♭
B♭7
E♭
bare. Gone, gone, Je - sus has ris - en, He's
do. Gone, gone, Je - sus has ris - en, As -
gone down to hell with the keys in His hand, He locked death a - way in e -
cend - ed to Heav - en to the Fath - er's right hand, He locked death a - way in e -
tern - i - ty's pri - son, The grave has been con - quered for ev - er - y
tern - i - ty's pri - son, The grave has been con - quered for ev - er - y
1.
2.
man.
man.

GOING, GOING, GONE

Words and Music
Sarah Hart and Joel Lindsey

Ab Db Ab

I was sat up-on the auc-tion block, But the bid-der would-n't of-fer a dime. They could
Are you wait-ing for some-one to come, And de-liv-er you from out of the blue? Are you

Db/Ab Ab Bb7 Eb7

see I was worn, I was dirt-y and torn, No they just kept pass-ing me by. Ah, but
sit-ting a-round with your head hang-ing down, Wond'-rin' why no-bod-y wants you? Well, I

Db/Ab Ab Db Bbm Ab/Eb

that's when a man stepped out of the crowd, He of-fered an in-cred-i-ble price. I could
know a man who is com-ing your way, With a heart full of heav-en-ly love, And the

Db D°7 Eb F7 Bbm Eb Ab **CHORUS**

hard-ly be-lieve how much He paid for me, 'Cause He bought me with His life. Well I'm
price that He'll pay is gon-na blow you a-way, 'Cause He'll buy you with His love.

Db7
Ab
go - ing, Ver - y soon I'm going to meet the man, Who paid the price for me, Yes, I'm
Db7
Bb Cm7 C#7 Bb/D Eb
go- ing, Ver- y soon I'm going to see the friend, Who bought my soul and set me free. He's gon- na
Ab
Ab7 Db
Bb7
come a- gain, And I'll be called up with Him, Be - fore you can say so long, In the
Db D°7 Eb F7 Bbm Eb Ab
snap of a fing - er, In the blink of an eye, I'll be go - ing, go - ing, gone.

ONE OUT OF TEN

Words and Music
Felecia Shifflett

A♭
E♭
I'm one out of ten, Oh, but I've come back a - gain, Be - cause
B♭7
E♭
some - where way down deep, You know you've made my soul com - plete, You've
A♭
E♭
done a work in me, Lord, may I work for You? Un -
B♭7
E♭
Fine
like the o - ther men, Lord, I'm one out of ten.

E♭
Now Je - sus looked a - round, As this one bound to lift Him
high, And there was such a long - ing, You could see it in the Sav - ior's
B♭7
E♭
A♭
eyes, For He knew that the nine, Would sym - bol - ize the church, Oh, but
E♭/G
A♭
E♭
B♭
B♭7
E♭
D.S. al Fine
that one out of ten, he want - ed more than just a touch. He said,Lord,

JUBILEE'S A COMING

Words and Music
Mosie Lister

G
C
F
2.
Gon - na be a shout - in' and sing - in' at the Jub - i - lee.
F
C7
Jub - i - lee's a com - in', Jub - i - lee's a com - in', Com - in' in the by and by,
C7
F
Gon - na go fly - in', gon - na go fly - in', Fly - in' up to the sky.
F
C7
When I see my Je - sus, When I see my Je - sus, Com - in' down af - ter me,

C7
F
Gon - na go to meet Him, Gon - na go to meet Him, What a glad Jub - i - lee. Jub - i -
B♭
F
lee, Jub - i - lee, I am go - ing to a hap - py Jub - i -
C
F
B♭
F
lee, Jub - i - lee, Jub - i - lee, I am
G7
C7
F
go - ing to a hap - py Jub - i - lee.

TWELVE GATES TO THE CITY

Words and Music
Unknown

G° C7
You know John said he saw the cit - y of great God, And the cen - ter was four square wide, He

C7 G7 C C7
stead - ied him - self, and then he looked a - gain, He saw Je - sus on the o - ther side. You know

C C7
my God spoke to the Rev - e - la - tor John, Said, John don't you write no more, He said

C7 G7 C
time has been, won't be no more, I'm gon - na close up Heav - en's door. There are

C7
F7
twelve gates to the cit-y, hal-le-lu, hal-le-lu, There are twelve gates to the cit-y, hal-le-lu,
F7
C
C7
Cm7
C
hal-le-lu. Oh what a beau-ti-ful cit-y, Oh what a beau-ti-ful cit-y,
C
G7
To Coda
C
G°
C7
I can see my Sav-ior stand-ing there. You know John was preach-in', preach-in' to the na-tion, That
C7
had ab-so-lute-ly no civ-il-i-za-tion, You read in your bi-ble, a-bout it in the gar-den,

G
C
God made heav - en, and earth cre - a - tion. He raised His head, He flashed His eyes, The
light from heav - en shone down, Then He stood on the banks of Jor - dan, He
G
3
C
D.S. al Coda
C
C7
looked and my God's work was done. There are there. Now when
3
C7
I get up in the cit - y, Gon - na see my moth - er, shake her hand, Gon - na

C7
see my fath - er, tour the cit - y, Gon - na ask my Lord for new shoes, Gon - na
G7
C
C7
walk all a - round Je - ru - sa - lem. Twelve gates to the cit - y, hal - le - lu,
C7
F7
hal - le - lu, There are twelve gates to the cit - y, hal - le - lu,
F7
C
C7
hal - le - lu, Oh what a beau - ti - ful cit - y,

C
Cm7
C
G7
Oh what a beau-ti-ful cit-y, I can see my Sav - ior stand - ing
C
G°
C7
there. There are three gates in the east, Three gates in the west,
F7
C
C7
Three gates in the north, Three gates in the south. There are three gates o-pen o-ver there, I
C7
got my sal-va-tion, and I won't be late, Three gates o-pen o-ver there, St. Pe -

C7
ter o - pen up those gold - en gates, You know, well, Twelve gates to the cit - y, hal - le - lu,
C7
F7
hal - le - lu, There are twelve gates to the cit - y, hal - le - lu,
F7
C
C7
hal - le - lu, Oh what a beau - ti - ful cit - y,
C
Cm7
C
G7
C
Oh what a beau - ti - ful cit - y, I can see my Sav - ior stand - ing there.